MacDonald, Bernell, 1948-
    The theories of fish

(Fiddlehead poetry books; 263)

Poems.
ISBN 0-920110-84-3 pa.

I. Title.   II. Series.

PS8575.D6T48   C811'.5'4   C79-094014-0
PR9199.3.M24T48

THE THEORIES OF FISH

by

BERNELL MacDONALD

Fiddlehead Poetry Books, 1979

To Franny and Davey with love

haunted houses

As boys we created fear for sport
imagined headless men
moving through darkness
behind windows
—we dared strike
with stones through glass
dared kick the doors ajar

Now though i am a grown man
i cannot stop the imagining—
glass in my windows
locks on my doors

anxiety attack

i am awakened
jump up
slap
my face
throw
water on
my head
take
two tran
quilizers
climb
back
into bed
knowing
there is
nothing
to be afraid of

and being afraid of it

poetic justice

Three months
ago
i immortalized
you
in poem
included
your name
in the title

Now
youve gone
and left me
for
another man

Suffer in hell bitch

ive erased
your name from the title

thanatophobia

i was today informed by my psychiatrist
that i have been suffering from a neurotic disorder:
the abnormal fear of death

i have pledged the remainder of my days
to the pursuit of acquiring
that normal degree
one requires

arachneophobia

a spider lives
in a hole
where my tub
adjoins
the bathroom wall

his omnipresence
has really got to me
his hairy little existence
must be terminated

somehow
i must call upon
all my courage

muster together
all my strengths

ignore him

wolverine

No man
without dying
believes
he is really
going to die

But
the night
the wolverine
attacked me
in my tent
i believed

Surviving then
was
a resurrection
and all i want to know

and can anybody tell me

what ever happened
to good old Lazarus

old photograph

my mother
is not yet seventeen

is most beautifully standing
before the open door
of my grandfather's house
posing
for this photograph

is most beautifully smiling
in the afternoon sun; i tell you
that moment
will never cease being

her feet are stained
with red Island clay

her long wild hair
moves with the summer breeze

and in the trees, trees
too incredibly high
for any photograph

birds are singing

follie du doute

Late at night
   nothing to do
   nowhere to go
wandering the deserted streets
of an unknown city
   i am being
   followed by a dog

Casually
i round a corner
   back
   suddenly flat
   against brick
the dog unsuspectingly . . .

HHYYAAA! GIT OUTTA HERE
YOU STUPID GODDAMN DOG!

and the dog yelps
runs down the street
disappears into the distance
   going godknowswhere now
   to do godknowswhat

And i . . .
wandering the deserted streets
of an unknown city

wonder
   if perhaps . . .

Perhaps i should follow him

aquariums

scientists and common sense
tell us it cannot be done—

> for the past two hours
> i have been staring in
> at my two new kuhli loaches
> who insist (writhing their bodies
> like little eels and bumping
> their noses against the sides)
> that they can pass through glass
> (and more
> that air is water)

—men and their truths standing
so long and staring into their aquariums
should not contradict the theories of fish

the Urological Argument

standing
alone
miles from anywhere
in the
middle
of a frozen lake
urinating
i have
the terrible
and awful feeling
that Somebody
is watching me

the jungle

The jungle is vast
and i am blind
                    stumbling
without reference point

But i am not lost

replay

watching the Olympic coverage
on television
a replay of yesterday's
cycling race

though i know
the inevitable outcome
i find myself
pounding my knees
biting my fists
rooting for
a predetermined loser

concerning editors

WHATS THE MATTER
WITH THEM ANYWAY!!

they reject my manuscripts

some make sly remarks
some reply two years later
others i never hear from

youd think i had forever
to become immortal

selves

i didnt mean
to hurt you darling

nor did i mean
to kick the dog

forgive me

i am a crowd

a thousand imposters
gather among me

observation

a hawk fleeing a
pack of sparrows—
lucky for the sparrows

dry spell

what happens
when all the poems are gone
really gone
a drought which
unlike the others
just wont end

if suddenly
i were empty
with no more poems for people
or myself
or just for their own sake

and when
even this poem's trick
wont work anymore

what then?

epitaph

you! the passerby who happened
    to glance upon my epitaph
        and stopped to catch your breath

read not this: "i am dead"
    (and having read run on) but instead:
        "when the hunted finds the hunter
            there can be no death"

red giant—white dwarf

lying
on my back
at the beach
squinting
at the sun
thinking
5 billion years
from now . . .

me
26 years old
with
a life expectancy
of 72
suddenly
really
PARANOID OVER IT

Witness

he tried so hard
to make me believe in *his* Christ
he forgot i was an aetheist

out of reach

watching her
seeing her
so beautifully
sleeping beside me
like that—

sometimes
its the thing already possessed
one covets the most

the skeptic

while hunting
we sighted
what appeared to me to be
nothing other than a sasquatch
running into the denser bush

"Did you see it too" i managed
to utter in rhetorical question

"There's no such thing" my friend replied
"And besides, it looked like a fake to me."

words

after a heated argument
this morning
and having all day
said nothing
to each other
tonight
in the same bed
facing different directions
both of us
feigning sleep
i wish one of us
would reconcile
that there could be
silence again

lycanthropy

Perhaps
it was the knapsack
and the long hair

Perhaps
it was because
it was an express
and the bus driver
shouldnt have stopped—

I dont know—

i just paid my fare and made my way
to the back the best i could

But
it wasnt until after
i seated myself and
pretended i was absorbed
by something beyond the window

did the occupants return
to their seats

retract their fangs

did the hair on the back
of their necks finally flatten

two minutes before the execution

the condemned,
asked what he would like
to drink
replied:
"Water please, a beer
would only make me crave another."

shoulders

winter. God is in his garden
pulling weeds in the snow
what God knows
is how the winter roses grow
I am among the cedar hedges
God does not see me
is working hard
God has broad shoulders

I am among the snowladen boughs
of cedar trees that grow around
the edge of God's garden
the roses are frozen
rattle
in a glass wind
God does not hear me

I am sneaking up on God
who is stooped over his winter roses
my feet are frozen

God turns to his house
snow falls from my blazer
God has high shoulders
leaves footprints

what if . . . (thinks the aetheist in one of his agnostic moods)

what if
there actually is a God
with a heaven
and a hell
and a judgement day
the whole bit

wont that
be a kick in the arse

aspirations

when i was little
    just for fun
        i tried to fly
like the birds

later
    it became an obsession
        and haunted my dreams

today
    i watch from my window
        birds tightropewalking
roof crests

ah . . . why bother with flight
when one can shoot pigeons
off roof tops

hay makes my balls itch

hay makes my balls itch
and thunderstorms play squash with my thoughts

if lightning should strike this barn
darling   i fear tomorrow
          will find me dead
                    naked
           and with a rash

out of my life

after five years . . .
i told her i didnt love her anymore

and she slapped me face
and walked out of my life
and i cried
because i couldnt feel the pain

the floormonster

its late
in bed my right arm dangles
                              over
its hand touches the floor

suddenly
          the realization
that something actually *could*
live under there

of course its ridiculous
i know that

but it has teeth
and lives off the flesh and blood
on live hands

poem

the tv guide is booked
with Elvis Presley movies
the radio stations jammed
with his songs

:

watching a movie now
seeing him
hearing him
i cant believe he's *really* dead

:so it is with us Immortals

porcupine

having plugged the porcupine
full of b.b.'s
(which hurt because b.b.'s cost 7 cents a pack)
he finally let go of the limb
and fell to the ground with
a hollow thud
whereupon we proceeded
(very professionally)
to smash his skull in
with the butts of our guns
then walked away not feeling a thing
because we knew
he would have done the same to us

In the CLOUD NINE HOTEL

no matter how hard you try
to simplify things
it always happens:

contemplating my beer
just minding my own business . . .

> "Lissin fella . . . Im no bum . . .
> juss wanna borrer a doller . . .
> paya back tomorrer . . . swear I will . . ."

"Sure . . . sure . . .
here . . . keep it . . ."

> "WELL THE HELL WITHYA THEN
> YA SONAVABITCH . . . IF YA WANNA BE
> LIKE THAT . . ."

and he turned
and stumbled away from my table
leaving me behind
with a skunky beer
my last dollar
and one more thing to contemplate

the poet's lot

i remember going with this girl
for the longest time
was even engaged to be married
to her
whose parents continuously
were trying to break us up
because being a poet
there was something "funny" about me
"obviously a fag"

here today

four years to have written this book
and now that its printed i fear . . .
why not simply have written
Bernie was here

CONTENTS

haunted houses 5
anxiety attack 6
poetic justice 7
thanatophobia 8
arachneophobia 9
wolverine 10
old photograph 11
follie du doute 12
aquariums 13
the Urological Argument 14
the jungle 5
replay 16
concerning editors 17
selves 18
observation 19
dry spell 20
epitaph 21
red giant—white dwarf 22
Witness 23
out of reach 24
the skeptic 25
words 26
lycanthropy 27
two minutes before the execution 28
shoulders 29
what if 30
aspirations 31
hay makes my balls itch 32
out of my life 33
the floormonster 34
poem 35
porcupine 36
in the CLOUD NINE HOTEL 37
the poet's lot 38
here today 39